WALKING CLOSE

PITSFORD WATER

Number Sixteen in the popular series of walking guides

Contents

Walk		Miles	Page No
1	Maidwell Dale	5¹/₂	4
2	Merry Tom Crossing	7³/₄	6
3	Hanging Houghton	5³/₄	8
4	Harrington Aerodrome	5	10
5	Pitsford Water (South)	6¹/₂	12
6	Pitsford Water (North)	9¹/₄	14
7	Old Poor's Gorse	8	17
8	Faxton Corner	4³/₄	20
9	Hardwick Wood	6¹/₄	22
10	Spectacle Lane	9	24

Walked, Written and Drawn by Clive Brown
© Clive Brown 2004 -2012

Published by Clive Brown
ISBN 978-1-907669-16-3

PLEASE
Take care of the countryside
Your leisure is someone's livelihood

Close gates
Start no fires
Keep away from livestock and animals
Do not stray from marked paths
Take litter home
Do not damage walls, hedgerows or fences
Cross only at stiles or gates
Protect plants, trees and wildlife
Keep dogs on leads
Respect crops, machinery and rural property
Do not contaminate water

Although not essential we recommend good walking boots; during hot weather take something to drink on the way. All walks can easily be negotiated by an averagely fit person. The routes have been recently walked and surveyed, changes can however occur, please follow any signed diversions. Some paths cross fields which are under cultivation. All distances and times are approximate.

The maps give an accurate portrayal of the area, but scale has however been sacrificed in some cases for the sake of clarity and to fit restrictions of page size.

Walking Close To have taken every care in the research and production of this guide but cannot be held responsible for the safety of anyone using them.

During very wet weather, parts of these walks may become impassable through flooding, check before starting out. Stiles and rights of way can get overgrown during the summer; folding secateurs are a useful addition to a walker's rucksack.

Thanks to Angela for help in production of these booklets

Views or comments?
walkingcloseto@yahoo.co.uk

Reproduced from Ordnance Survey Mapping on behalf of The Controller of Her Majesty's Stationery Office. © Crown Copyright License No. 100037980.

16:C

Walking Close to Pitsford Water

Situated in the southern part of the triangle formed by the A14, the A43 and the A508, Pitsford Water is, along with Rutland Water and Grafham Water, part of Anglian Water's Ruthamford water supply network supplying millions of gallons daily to the major towns of the East Midlands.

The reservoir, which was opened in 1956 by the Queen Mother, is split into two halves by the causeway between Brixworth and Holcot. The northern half is given over to wildlife in the form of a large nature reserve. A permit, available from the car park nearest to Holcot, is required to visit the bird hides on either shore. Walk no 6 in this booklet takes a wide route around the lake, through fields, along tracks and bridleways.

The southern half, while still home to large numbers of waterfowl and other wildlife, is the centre for a wide range of leisure and water based activities. Access is easy from the car parks either end of the causeway, north of Pitsford village and Brixworth Country Park. A hardcore path circles the lake connecting each of these car parks and walk no 5 makes use of this path as well as rights of way further away from the shore.

The other walks contained in this booklet use paths, bridleways, rights of way and national recreational paths. There is very little walking on roads except where unavoidable. Most walking is on firm, good quality paths which are well marked and signposted. Paths may cross fields under cultivation and some are more obscure and less well directed; the detailed instructions will guide past these points. Some of the walks are in countryside already popular with walkers; others are in areas less popular and perhaps less accessible.

Walk nos 1,2,3 and 4 make use of the Brampton Valley Way which is a linear park, cycle way and footpath running for fourteen miles along the trackbed of the former railway between Northampton and Market Harborough. After the demise of the railway in 1981 it was purchased by Northamptonshire council and developed for recreational use. The Northampton and Lamport Railway runs steam and vintage rolling stock, and is operated by enthusiasts on the southern section of the Way between Boughton and Merry Tom Crossing (walk no 2).

We feel that it would be difficult to get lost with the instructions and maps provided, but recommend carrying an Ordnance Survey map. Explorer maps are best No. 223 covers all but a small section of walk no 9 which is on Map no 224, Landranger Nos. 141 & 152 cover at a smaller scale. Roads, geographical features and buildings, not on our map but visible from the walk, can be easily identified.

1 Maidwell Dale

5$^1/_2$ Miles   2$^1/_2$ Hours

Park in the Draughton Crossing car park and picnic area. Part of the Brampton Valley Way, east of the A508 between Maidwell and Draughton. Picnic tables only, ice creams peak times.

1   Walk along the Brampton Valley Way to the north for three quarters of a mile to the signpost at a crossroads; turn left, signposted Maidwell village, on the farm track between fields. Follow the track left and bear right at the signpost along the hedged byway and continue to the road.

2   Turn right at the road then almost immediate left signposted to Haselbech with Scotland Wood to the right. After close to a mile turn left at the Haselbech Grange Lorry Entrance. Go through the boundary ahead, after 100yds take a left hand diagonal to a hidden set of steps and cross the footbridge in a hedge gap, this field may be under cultivation but a track should be well marked within any crop. Bear right at the marker post and continue down the field edge with the hedge and dyke to right.

3   Turn left and immediate right at the trees down a sunken farm road then turn left on an easy to miss path through the trees to a signpost. Turn left and keep on this path on the edge of the trees above Maidwell Dale with the field at head height on the right. After half a mile bear right at the bottom of some steps.

4   Emerging from the woods follow the field edge left with the hedge then the fence to the left. Turn left then right with the fence, follow the left hand field edge and go left through the gap between the wall and the hedge. Turn right on the tarmac drive; follow it left at the house and walk around the gates.

5   Just past the green triangle turn left at the signpost through the trees, bear right over the footbridge and continue ahead with the hedge to the left. Cross the stile and keep direction over another stile and a narrow field to a stile between a brick shed and a wooden fence. Go down the enclosed path around the garden and up to the road in Maidwell. Walk across the busy A508.

6   Go straight on along the road signposted Draughton and follow the road left then right. As the road swings left at the church carry straight on along the enclosed drive, bear slight left through the kissing gate up to the marker post; turn right along the left hand field edge over stiles and footbridge. Bear right over another stile and join the Brampton Valley Way to the right under the skeletal footbridge back to the Draughton Crossing and your vehicle.

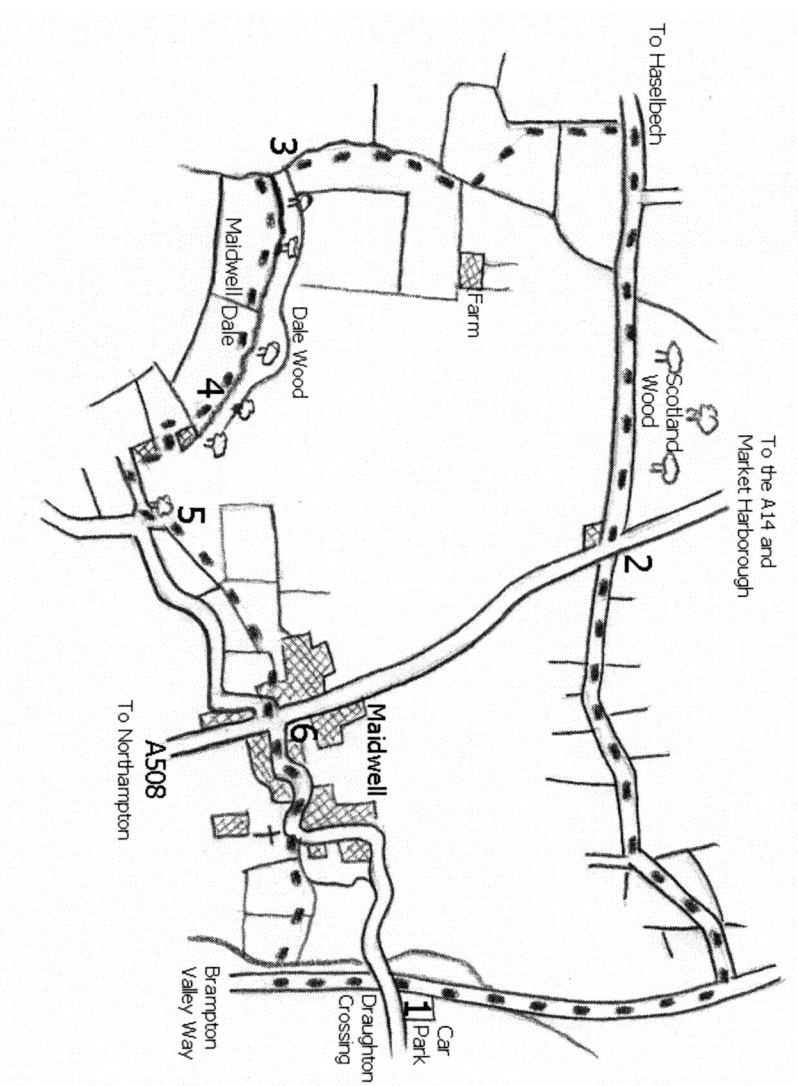

Large flocks of Canada Geese are usually around Pitsford Water. They are opportunistic birds, soon appearing if there is any chance of free food, particularly the car park at the western end of the causeway. They are not native to the British Isles, having been artificially introduced in the 17th Century. Man made reservoirs like Pitsford Water and disused gravel pits seem to provide them with an ideal habitat. While not actually tame they are very tolerant of human presence.

2   Merry Tom Crossing

7³/₄ Miles   3¹/₂ Hours

Park at Brixworth Country Park (pay and display), toilets, café, shop and picnic/barbeque area.

1 Follow the path with the hedge to the right down towards the reservoir and turn right through the gap in the bottom corner. Go along the path between the trees and the fence, bear left at the gate and walk across the dam. Turn left at the end through the gate and follow the shore, bear right along the inlet to a gate.

2 Turn right up this narrow tarmac lane, past a car park and into Pitsford village. Turn left at the green triangle junction towards Moulton and follow the road out of the village. Bear left with the road and turn almost immediate right at the signpost through the kissing gate.

3 Walk down the track between the hedge and the embankment, go through the gap in the corner and continue on the left hand field edge with the hedge to the left. Turn left through the gap at the bottom for 50yds and turn right over the double stile, bear left over the field and the stile at the signpost.

4 Turn right along the hedged path uphill and continue as it becomes a road all the way to the junction in Boughton village. Go straight on along Vyse Road and turn left into Humfrey Lane; turn almost immediate right down a wide fenced path. Turn right at the road and walk straight on at the junction up to the A508.

5 At the roundabout turn right and follow the roadside path for 600yds to the signpost for the Brampton Valley Way, turn left along this tarmac farm road. Walk past Grange Farm, keep direction on the path beyond and then the right hand field edge, go through the gate onto the Brampton Valley Way and turn right.

6 Continue on the path by the side of the Northampton and Lamport Railway. Cross the railway just past the sidings and carry on with the railway track now to the left. When the railway track stops cross the bridge and walk up to the signpost at Merry Tom Crossing; turn right between the concrete gateposts.

7 Walk past the farm and continue on this stony farm road all the way to the road near Brixworth. Turn right along the roadside path and cross the A508 at the roundabout. Carry on ahead (signposted Country Park) and turn left back to the car park and your vehicle.

Merry Tom was a hunter belonging to the first Lord Spencer; it was killed attempting to jump over the brook. The horse is buried nearby still wearing its saddle and harness.

16:C

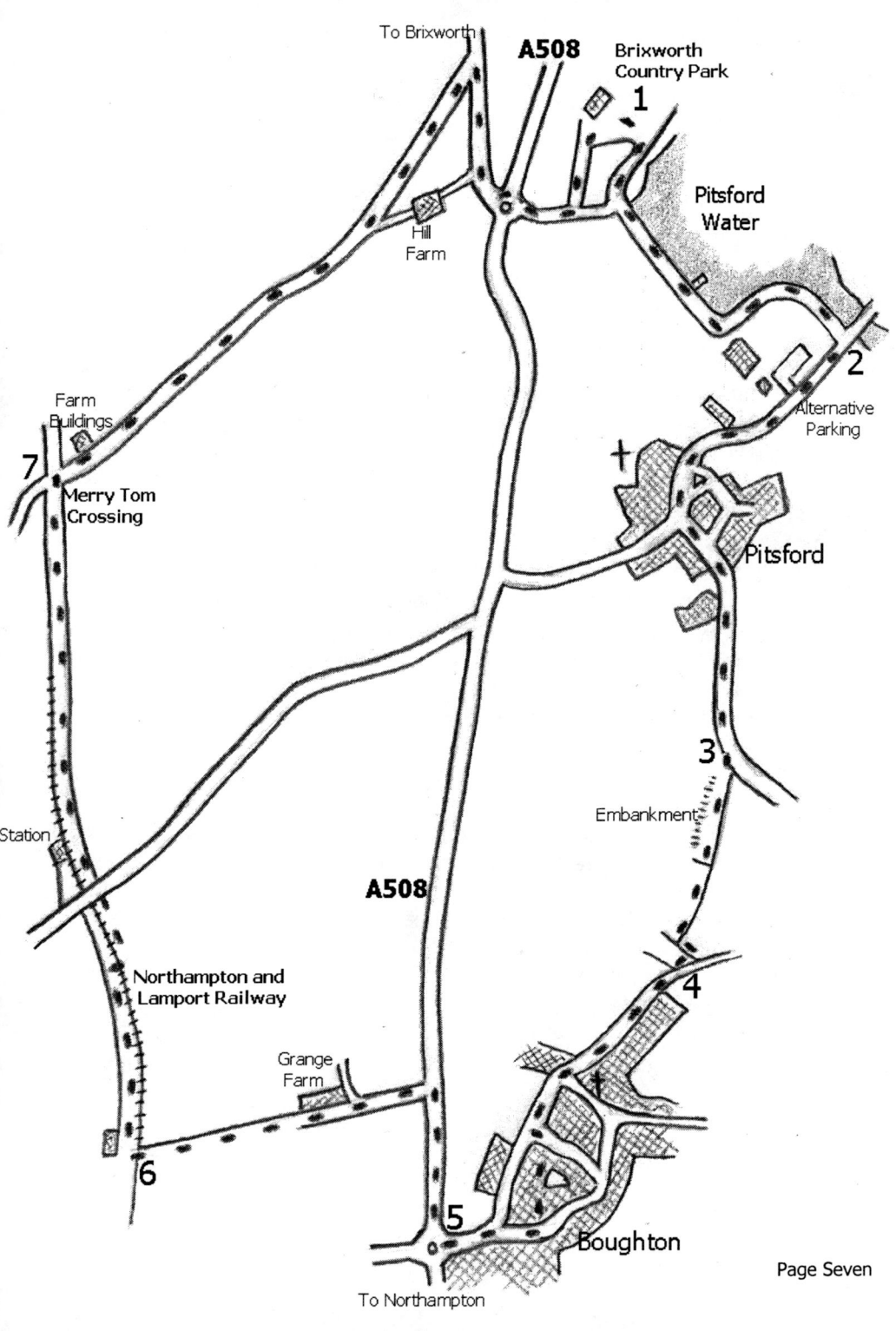

3 Hanging Houghton

5³/₄ Miles   2¹/₂ Hours

Park in either of the lay-bys each side of the A508 just north of Hanging Houghton. No facilities, pub (half a mile north) the 'Lamport Swan'.

1   Walk back to the junction and turn right into Hanging Houghton village, bear left at the end past the 'Unsuitable for Motors' sign and follow the narrow tarmac road as its surface gradually deteriorates, down to the Brampton Valley Way at Houghton Crossing.

2   Continue straight on along the farm track past the barn. This track leads eventually to a signpost in front of the trees at the top of a low rise.

3   Turn right along the byway with the hedge to the left, keep direction, bearing left at the hedge gap at the corner of the second field and carry on with hedge now to the right. The track goes into a hedged lane and bears right past a house.

4   At the four way signpost, turn right along the right hand field edge, as the field edge swings right go right through a wide hedge gap and continue direction with the hedge now left. Bear left through the first hedge gap (confirmed by the sign on the opposite side). Keep direction bearing left then right within the third field. Go up and over the hill and turn right at the bottom of the slope. Turn left through the gate and walk past the trees, cross the Brampton Valley Way and continue uphill to the A508.

5   Turn right along the grass verge and the roadside path through Lamport village, (the walk may be ended here by continuing straight on to the lay-by, in sight ahead). Just past the entrance to Lamport Hall, turn left at the signpost, go through the gate and down the hardcore track between the field and the trees. Carry on through the next gate and follow the directional arrow across the field (a track should be visible) towards the wide hedge gap.

6   Before the gap is reached turn right on what should be a marked crossroads of paths to an overgrown and easily missed gap; on the other side turn right along the field edge track back to the A508. Turn right back to the lay-by and your vehicle.

The Isham family, originally from the village of the same name near Kettering, owned several properties in the vicinity including Lamport Hall and Pytchley Hall. The 'Lamport Swan' pub reflects their use of this bird as a family emblem.

16:C

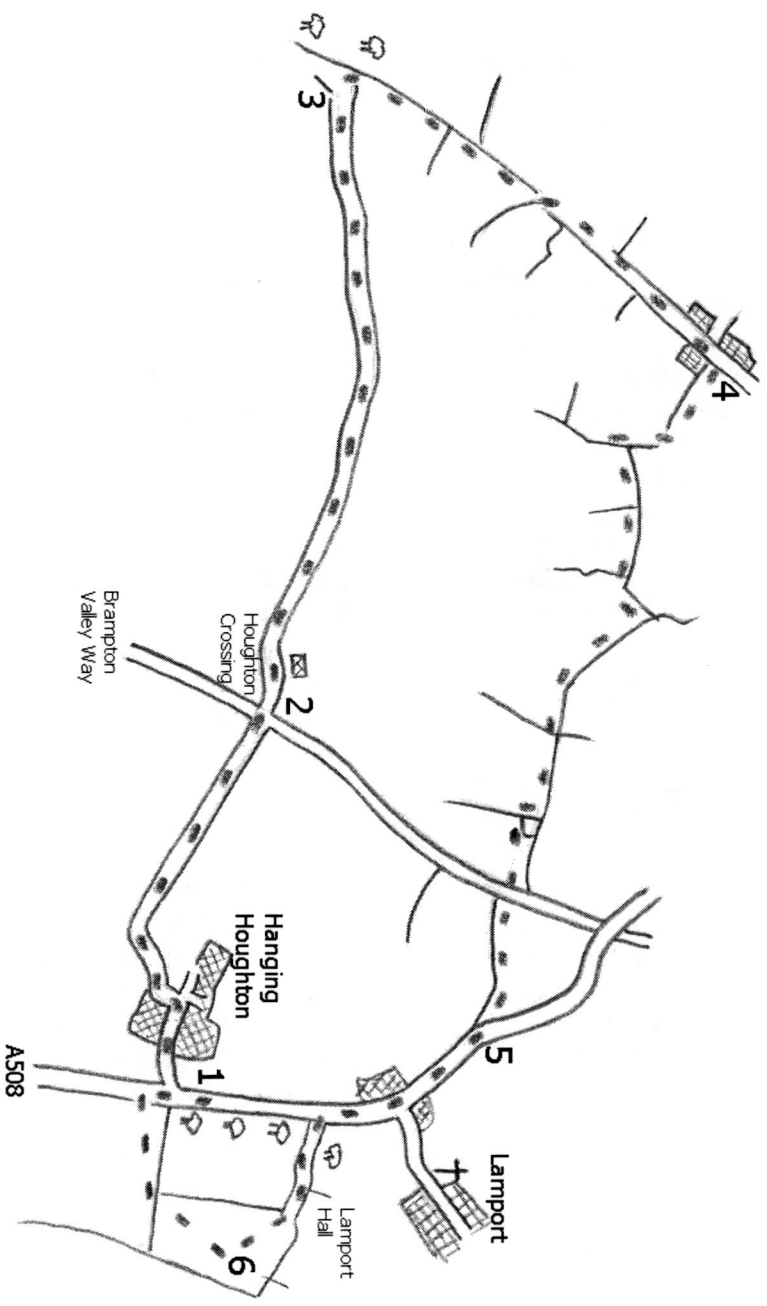

4   Harrington Aerodrome

5 Miles   2$^1/_2$ Hours

Park in the Draughton Crossing car park and picnic area. Part of the Brampton Valley Way, east of the A508 between Maidwell and Draughton. Picnic tables only, ice creams peak times.

1   Walk south from the car park along the Brampton Valley Way for a quarter of a mile. At the foot of the derelict skeletal iron footbridge turn right over the stile, bear right along the track and go over the double stile/footbridge. Carry on up the right hand field edge and bear left to the second right hand corner.
2   Go through the kissing gate to the road at the church in Maidwell and turn right, just before the road swings right again turn left and bear right through a metal gate. Follow this farm track bearing right to a stile left of the opposite corner; continue ahead on the track at the left hand field edge.
3   Bear right at the marker post along the track between fields to the Brampton Valley Way. Keep direction on the other side between trees and ahead over the field on a track which should be well marked if the field is under cultivation. Keep direction along the field edge and the farm track with the hedge to the left.
4   At the A14, bear right between trees along the tarmac byway past the aviation Museum and the trees of Blue Covert. As the main byway turns left go straight on through the trees on a less substantial path.
5   Turn right to find the concrete perimeter road of the disused Harrington Aerodrome and walk along it for just over a mile to the road.
6   Turn right downhill, past the church to the junction in Draughton village; go straight on through the gateway ahead down the tree lined drive. Cross stiles either side of the small field and keep direction over the field ahead; cross the boundary left of the pond on the almost hidden path and go over the field to the Brampton Valley Way at the derelict footbridge. Turn right back to the car park and your vehicle.

The airfield was used in the Second World War by the United States Air Force. A unit based here, nicknamed the 'Carpetbaggers' used black painted Liberator aircraft to despatch secret agents and supplies to occupied Europe.

16:C

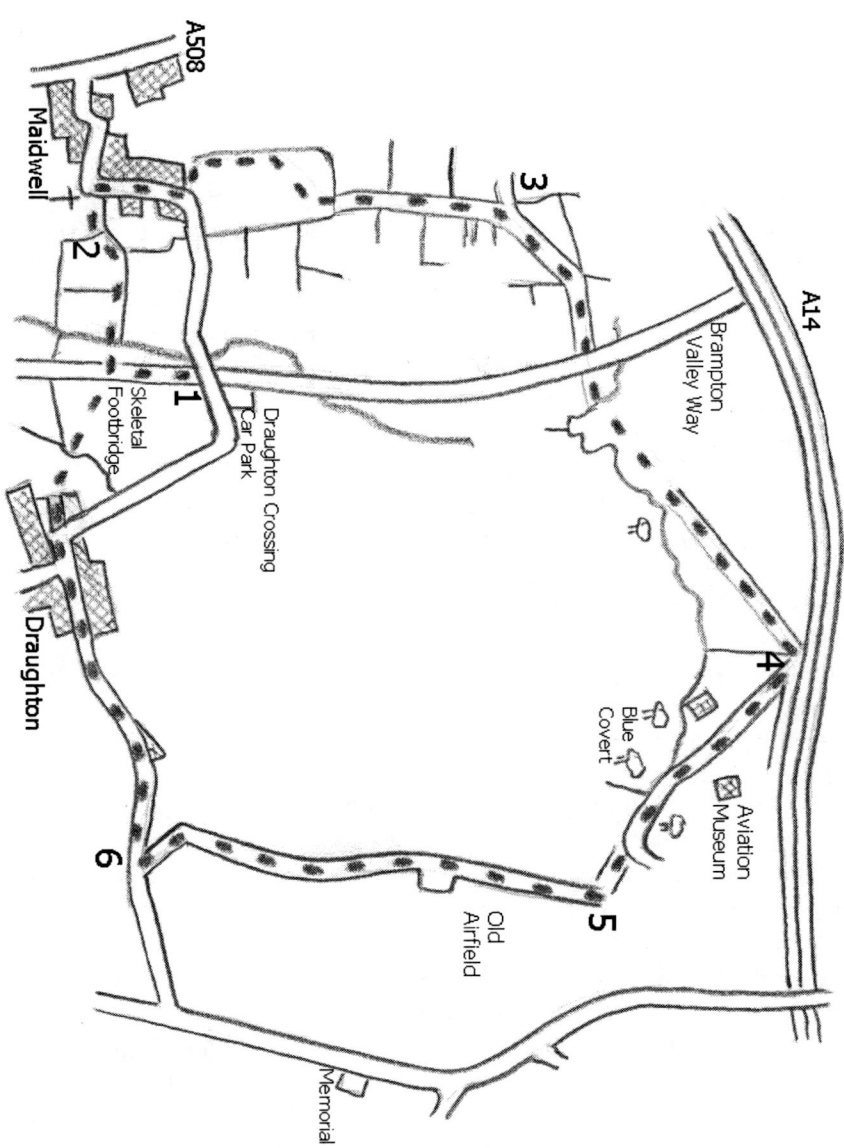

5 Pitsford Water (South)

6½ Miles 3¼ Hours

Park in the car park of Brixworth Country Park off the A508 south of Brixworth (Pay and display). Toilets, Café, visitor Centre and picnic area.

1 Start from the front of the visitor centre and turn left along the tarmac lakeside path. Follow the path for just over a mile and a half to a green footpath signpost for Brixworth and Scaldwell. Go through the gate and up the slope on the right hand field edge, continue through the next kissing gate and walk up to the road.

2 Turn right through the kissing gate and follow the field edge parallel to the road, turn left through the gate at the end and turn right along the roadside verge. Carry on downhill over the causeway and up the slope the other side.

3 Just after the Holcot sign, turn right over a stile and take a right hand diagonal over this field which should have a track visible within any crop. Cross the stile and follow the left hand field edge into the dip. Go over the footbridge, turn right through the gap then left uphill with the hedge to the left. Cross the access road, bear right along the left hand hedge to a stile in front of the show jump and cross.

4 Go straight over the field on a track which should be visible within any crop to a marker post, turn right and follow the field edge into the dip. Go through the kissing gates and over the footbridge, keep direction up the slope parallel with the telegraph poles to a hedge gap. Carry on through the trees, over the footbridge and the corner of the next field.

5 Continue over the more substantial footbridge and keep going on the left hand field edge, turn right in the corner for 50yds then turn left through two kissing gates. Maintain direction through more kissing gates, over the footbridge and a boundary bearing right towards half-timbered houses.

6 Turn left on the tarmac drive and follow as it swings right downhill over the causeway. Just on the far side turn right through a narrow metal gate.

7 Keep on this path as it turns left then right over the dam. Walk past the sailing club entrance turn right through a gate down the path between the trees and the fence. Turn left at the signpost back to the car park and your vehicle.

Brixworth church was built around 680; the bricks used in the main church are thought to have been recycled from derelict Roman buildings in the area.

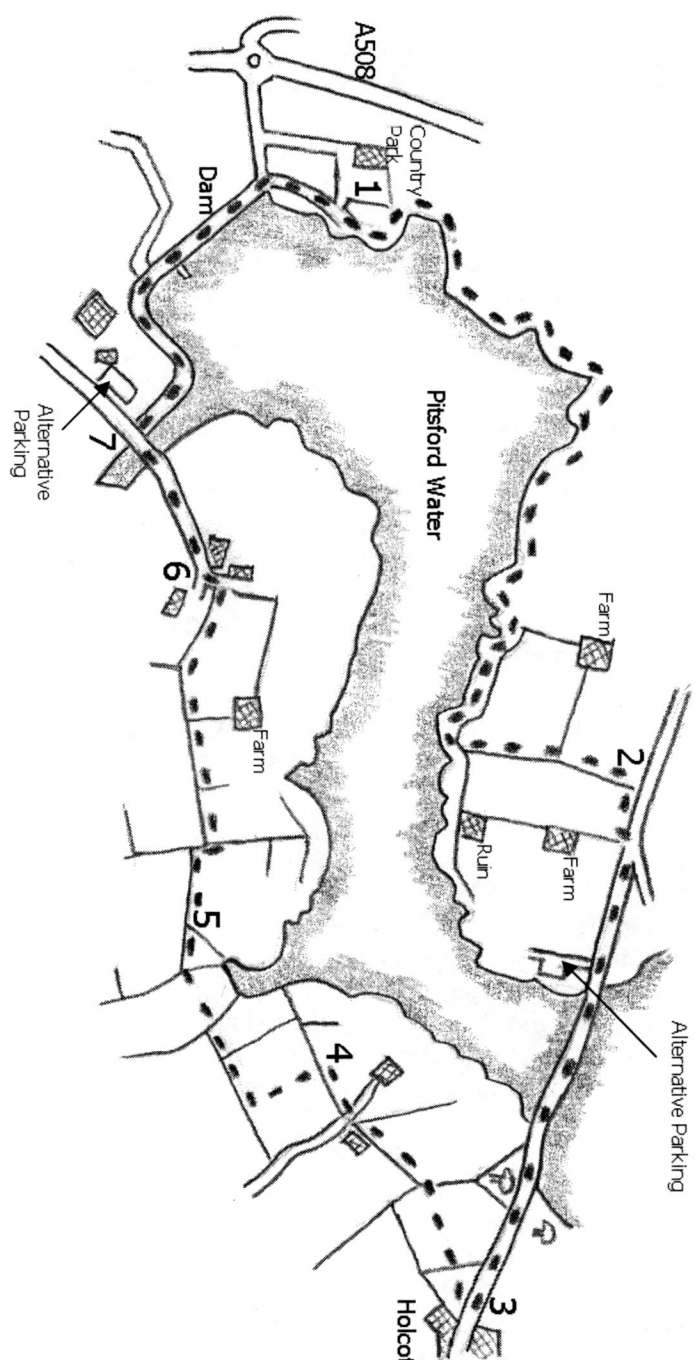

Page Thirteen

6 Pitsford Water (North)

9¼ Miles   4½ Hours

See larger scale map on Page Sixteen

Park in the car park at the western end of the causeway separating the two halves of the reservoir half a mile west of Holcot. No facilities, ice cream and hot drinks at busy times.

1 Go out of the entrance, cross the road and turn left along the roadside verge. After a third of a mile turn sharp right downhill past a barrier on a tarmac path. Turn left at the footpath sign attached to a tree over a stile, continue on the left hand field edge and bear left at the end of the second field keeping the fence on the left. Go through the gate and take a right hand diagonal to the opposite corner.

2 Cross the stile and bear left diverging from the trees, continue over the stile on the right of the two metal gates and up the hedged track. Go through the gate by the farm and carry on along the gravely road, as it swings left take the grassy overgrown track straight on and cross a stile to the left. Walk over the field **(A)** and the short piece of road into Scaldwell.

3 At the T-junction turn right down the slope and cross the stile; take a right hand diagonal down to the opposite corner, go over the footbridge and bear left down the fenced path. Step right over the stile and cross the field diagonally left over a stile **(B)** and on to the farm road. Turn right and cross the stile left of the two white gates; walk across the farmyard past the corner of the barn **(C)** and over the stile ahead.

4 Keep direction through the wide hedge gap and follow the right hand field edge down to the stile/footbridge in the bottom of the dip **(D)**. Bear left to the hedge gap at the top left, maintain direction through the metal gate and follow the right hand field edge to a stile and cross. Bear left over the next stile; keep direction over the field and cross the stile onto on to the road.

5 Turn right into Old village, walk through the village to Bridle Road and turn right. Go up to the signpost at the end of the wall on the left and cross the field on a slight diagonal to a stile/gate at the opposite corner. Maintain direction over the

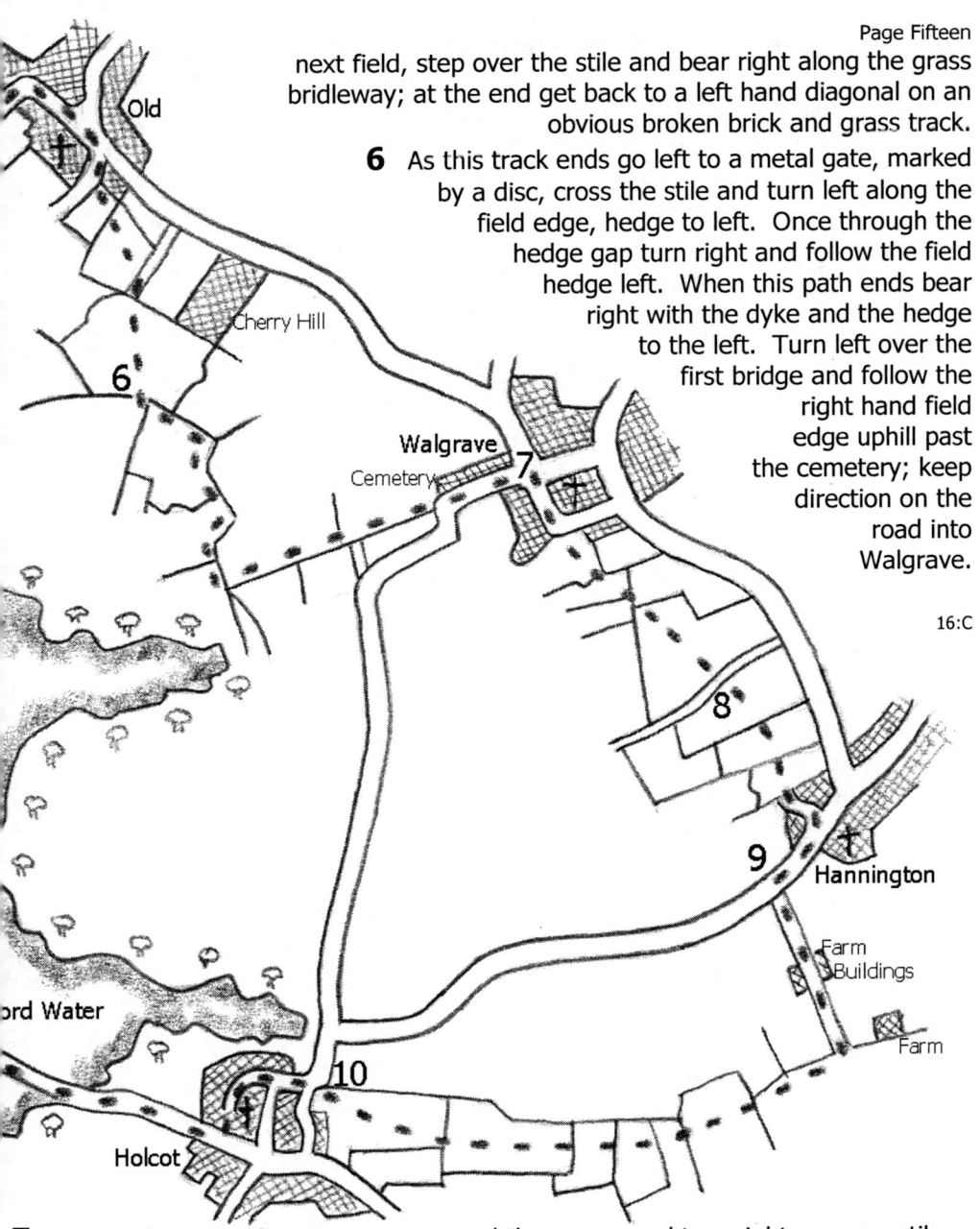

next field, step over the stile and bear right along the grass bridleway; at the end get back to a left hand diagonal on an obvious broken brick and grass track.

6 As this track ends go left to a metal gate, marked by a disc, cross the stile and turn left along the field edge, hedge to left. Once through the hedge gap turn right and follow the field hedge left. When this path ends bear right with the dyke and the hedge to the left. Turn left over the first bridge and follow the right hand field edge uphill past the cemetery; keep direction on the road into Walgrave.

7 Turn right into Bakers Lane, go around the corner and turn right across a stile just before the stone cottage. Walk down the left hand field edge, cross the footbridge and bear left to the top left corner. Cross this stile and the corner of the field to the next stile, carry on over the next field (a track should be visible through any crop); go through the hedge gap and over the byway.
Completed on the next Page (Sixteen)

Completion of 6 Pitsford Water (North) from the previous Page

8 Keep direction across the next two fields, step over the stile and continue through the high metal gate. Carry on uphill between the wall and the fence through the second high metal gate. Bear left up to the road in Hannington and turn right at the church, follow the road to a gate on the left marked by a disc.

9 Turn left along the track between the farm buildings; go through the boundary and over the bridge. Walk 100yds uphill into the field and turn right, back down to the corner. Follow the right hand field edge with the dyke to the right through two boundaries and over a double stile (only the concrete step remains of the second!) Continue through a hedge gap and straight over the next field; cross the footbridge and bear slight right over the stile ahead. Keep direction over the long field.

10 Go through the gate in the corner and turn left into Holcot. Walk ahead into Rectory Lane, follow left then right and turn left along the alleyway. At the bottom turn right on the road out of the village down the hill and across the causeway to the car park and your vehicle.

Larger scale map of the Scaldwell to Old section

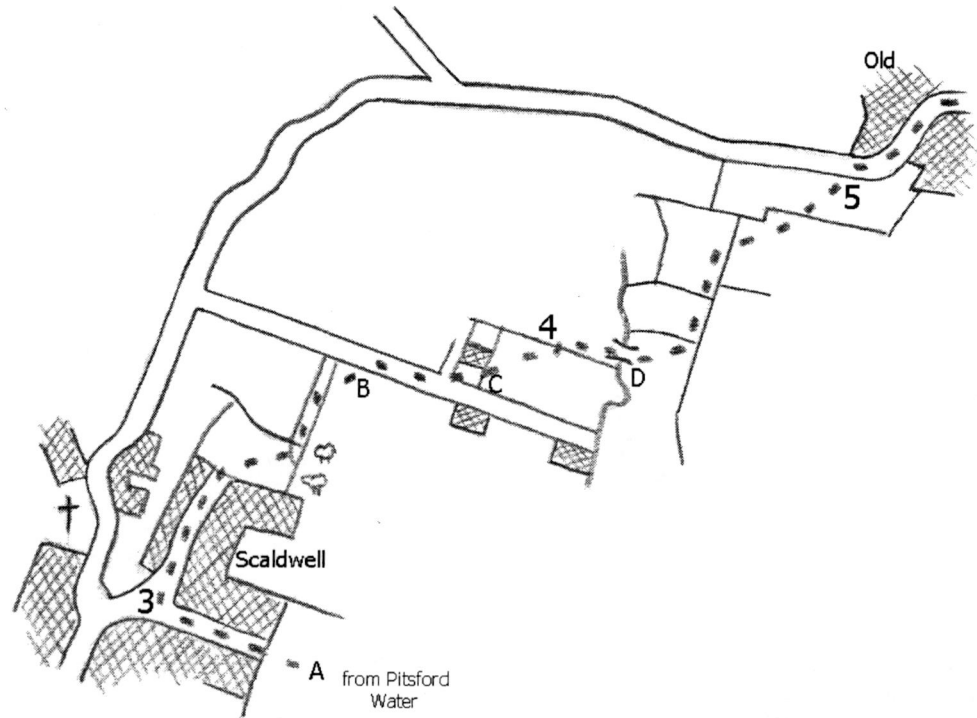

The map makes it look complicated; on the ground it's easy to follow!

7   Old Poor's Gorse

8 Miles   4 Hours

Find a parking space in Old village. Pub 'The White Horse', no other facilities.

1   Facing 'The White Horse' turn right and follow the road left then right; at the derestriction signs turn left over the stile **(A)**, head slight right and cross the next stile. Take a sharper right to the double stile on the right hand edge, step over and turn left; follow the left hand field edge through the gate and the next metal gate slight right. Bear sharper right across the stile/footbridge over the stream.

2   Walk up the left hand field edge, turn left through the gate and bear diagonally right over the field to the left hand corner of the barn. Continue through the gate and along the hardcore road, turn left over a stile **(B)** and cross to a stile hidden in the right hand hedge. Turn left down a fenced path and bear right over the footbridge; maintain direction up the slope and along the road into Scaldwell.

3   At the village green turn right past the church along Old Road. At the signpost for Lamport turn left/straight on past the houses and over the stile **(C)**, this field may be under cultivation but a track should be well marked through any crop. Go through the gate and keep direction past two marker posts at the field intersection and over the next field to the top left corner. Follow the farm track left with the hedge on the right. At the boundary bear right, a track should be visible, an unmarked crossroads of paths should also be visible after 100 to 150yds, turn right here.

4   Continue through the wooden gate and along the right hand edge of the next field with the fence to the right. Go through the gate near the house and turn right along the road for 30yds then turn left past the signpost back to the original direction along the grass bridleway. Carry on through a gate and down a narrow tree lined path and through the next narrow gate into a field.

The maps and completion of the text are on the following Pages

7 Old Poor's Gorse continued from the previous Page

5 Turn right along the right hand field edge. Go through a metal gate and continue on the field edge into a dip. As the ground rises again bear left then right through a metal gate; bear left at the marker post, after 100yds go through the gate and turn right along the field edge with the fence and trees to the right. Keep direction through the green gate and follow the tarmac drive ahead to the road.

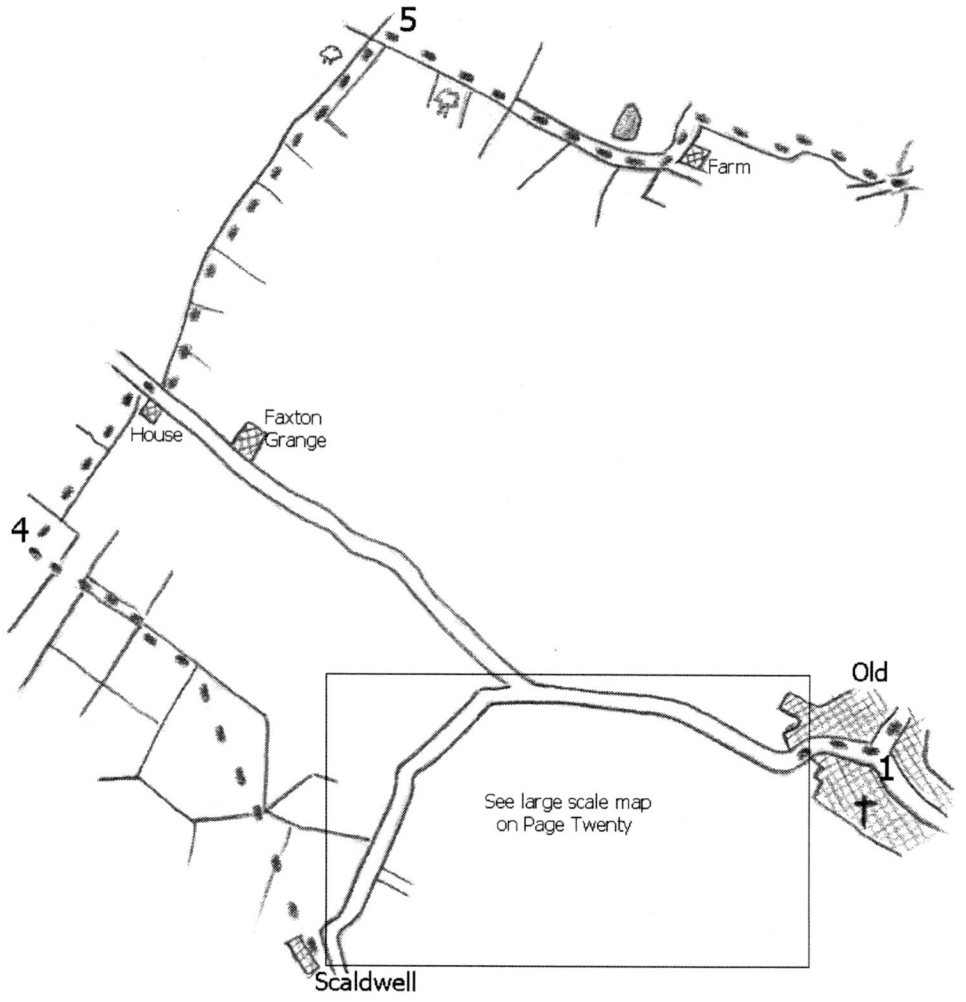

6 Cross and continue on the bridleway ahead with the hedge to the right, pass by the green gate to a corner that juts out. Bear left over the field (a track should be visible) to the gap and follow the hardcore farm track to the road.

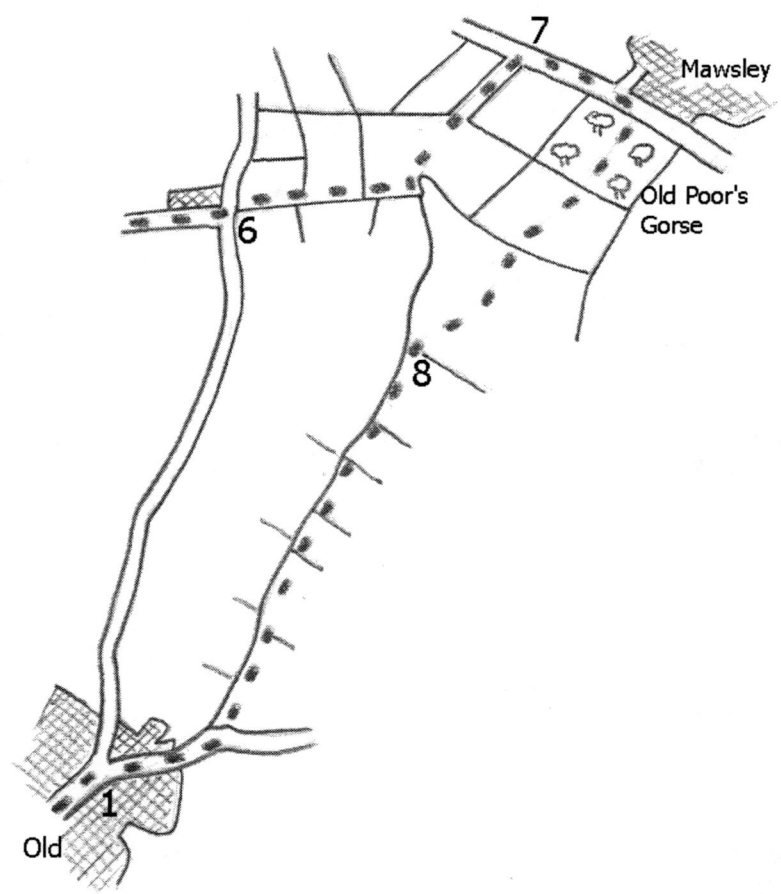

7 Bear right for a quarter of a mile, with the new village of Mawsley to the left. Just past the aerial turn right over a stile at the footpath sign and walk through Old Poor's Gorse. Come out of the trees and keep direction over the field ahead (track should be visible). Cross the footbridge at the hedge gap, walk halfway over the next field and bear right to the top right corner.

8 Carry on ahead along this right hand field edge for exactly a mile into the narrow corner of a field. Cross the stile in the hedge and turn right into Old to find your vehicle,

Larger scale map of the Old to Scaldwell section.
The map makes it look complicated; on the ground it's easy to follow!

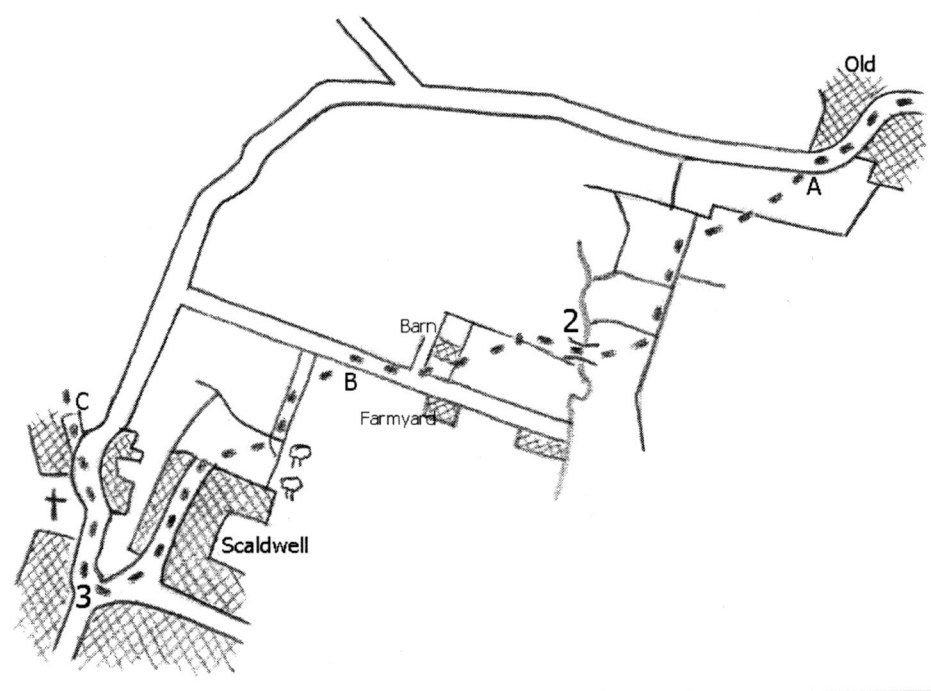

8   Faxton Corner

4³/₄ Miles   2¹/₄ Hours

Park on the wide grass verge alongside Faxton Corner. No facilities. Start from the south east corner (grid ref 791775).

1 Walk along to the south east tip of Faxton Corner and turn right at the bridleway sign down the right hand field edge. Keep direction from the gate over the bridge on an undefined track about halfway between Stonegrove Spinney on the right and the solitary tree on the left to a gateway marked by a disc, right of the corner ahead. Go through and follow the left hand edge of the field through a wide gap at the next boundary to a gate in the corner.

2 Go through the gate marked by discs, turn left for 10yds and continue on the left hand field edge. Maintain direction through two more gates, then go through a metal gate and down the track between hedges with the tall conifers to the right.

3 Bear right at the end, past the marker post, through the gate and along the farm track with the hedge to the left, bearing right over the stream and past the large pond. Carry on uphill through the gate and past the small stand of trees.

4 In the corner turn right, continue with the trees of Short Wood to the left. As the wood ends bear right at a marker post, then left through a hedge gap at the next marker post. Walk along this right hand field edge to a gap and go up the short, sharp slope. Turn left up to the corner and turn right; follow the field edge and bear left over the footbridge.

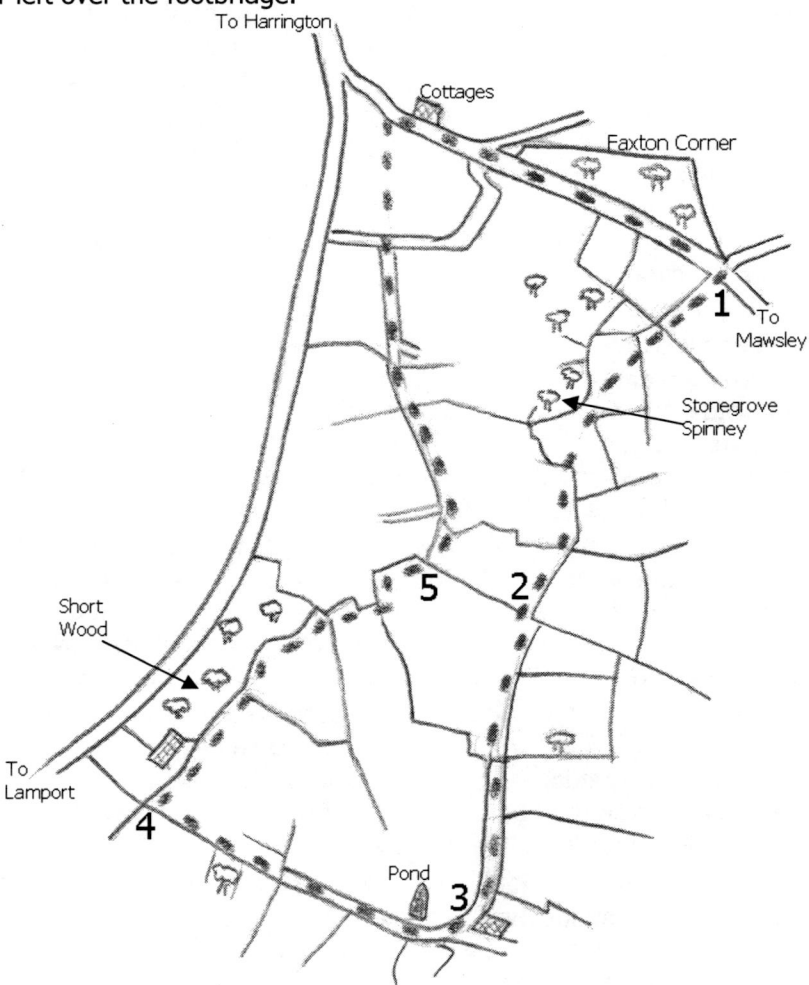

5 Keep direction on the left hand edge of two fields and the concrete farm road with the hedge to the right. As this farm road swings right maintain direction over the field ahead, this field may be under cultivation but a path should be well marked within any crop, to the signpost left of the line of cottages. At the road turn right back to Faxton Corner and your vehicle.

9 Hardwick Wood   10-7-16

6¼ Miles   3 Hours

Park in the lay-by (Grid Reference SP 827726) on the southbound side of the A43, a third of a mile north of the crossroads for Hannington and Orlingbury, no facilities, pub 'Henrys' (the Old Red House) and a Shell petrol station at the crossroads.

1   Facing the Northampton (southern) direction turn left at the signpost at the end of the lay-by. Walk up the bridleway with the hedge to the right, bear left through the wide hedge gap and cross the field ahead diagonally to the opposite corner. Turn sharp right here, along the left hand edge of this same field with the hedge to the left. Keep direction through two metal gates, past the farmhouse to the corner of the wood; bear right on the edge of the field around the wood to the road.

2   Turn left and walk for nearly two thirds of a mile to the signpost just short of the farm. Turn right and cross the field, diverging from the hedge on what should be a well marked track within any crop (not the farm track parallel to the hedge) and cross the footbridge in the dip. Turn right, then left in the corner and continue uphill past a marker post and through a narrow hedge gap. Maintain direction (a path should be visible) passing left of the tree circled pond.

3   Cross the road and step over the stile nearly opposite, bear right and cross the footbridge close to the garden. Turn right for 30yds alongside the hedgerow and bear left over the field with the shallow dyke to the left. Go through the gap, bear left with the hedge to the left and continue through the gate marked by a disc. Bear right along the edge of Hardwick Wood and keep direction to the A43.

4   Cross over carefully and turn left along the grass verge. Turn right over the stile at the first footpath sign, carry on up the right hand field edge with the hedge to the right through a boundary and follow the hedge left. Bear right through the wide gap and continue on the right hand edge of the field. Go down the slope and ahead along a sunken tree lined path into Hannington village.

5   Turn left along Main Street for 120yds and cross the stile and footbridge at the bottom of the slope. Continue over the stile at the top, bear left along the field edge and descend to the road. Cross and carry on ahead along the path between hedges and fences. Turn right over a stile opposite a substantial iron gate and carry on diagonally with the fence to the right over two stiles to the green bridleway.

6   Turn right up to the road and continue direction on the left hand field edges, then with conifers to the right all the way back to the A43. Turn right the short distance to your vehicle in the lay-by.

16:C

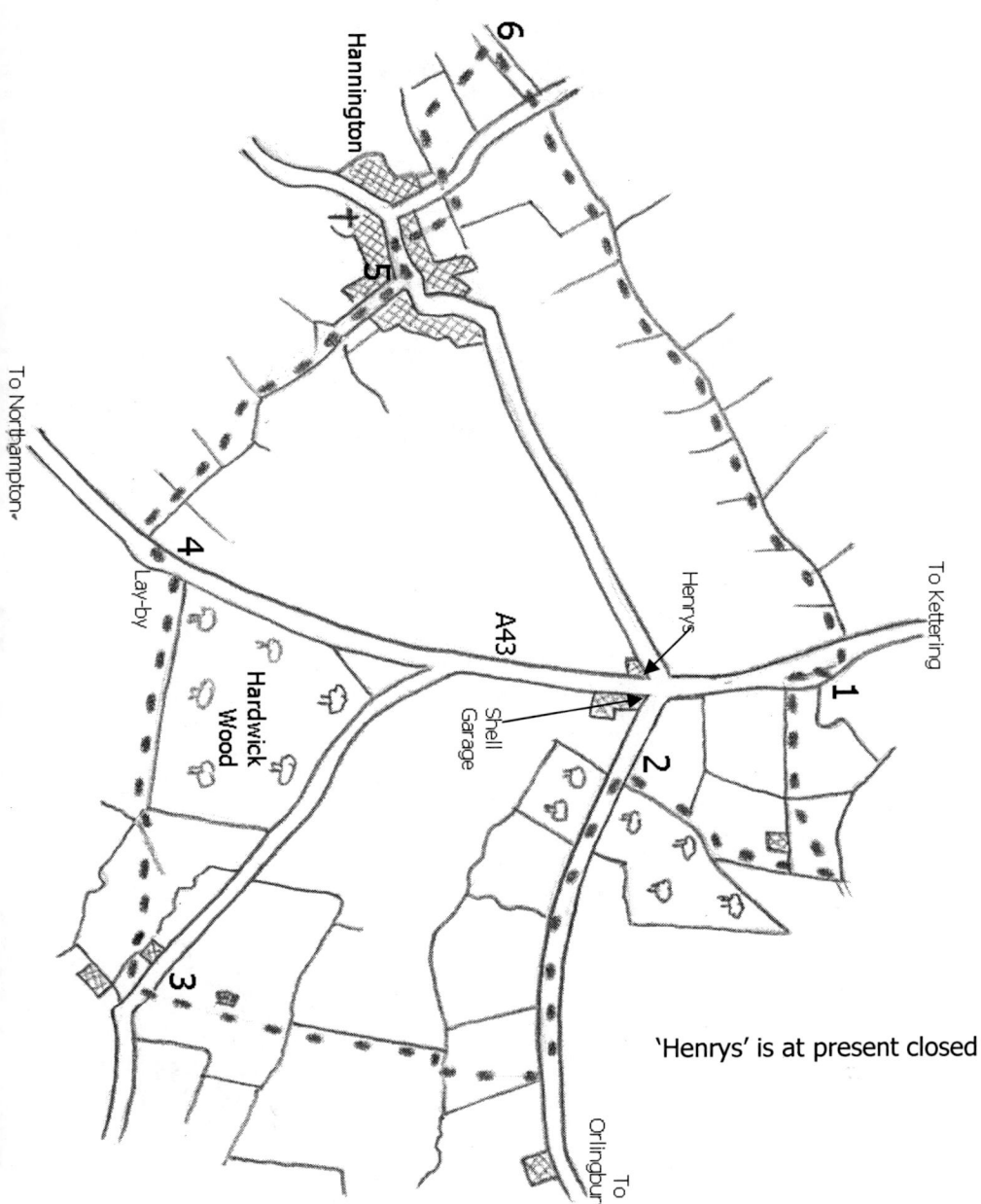

'Henrys' is at present closed

The road between Northampton and Kettering, later classified as the A43, did not exist until 1819. It was built to shorten the roundabout journey to Stamford via Oundle. This late date of construction explains the fairly straight route and the fact there are no villages between Moulton and Broughton.

10 Spectacle Lane

9 Miles   4¹/₄ Hours

Park in the car park north of Pitsford village, toilets (which may not be unlocked) no other facilities.

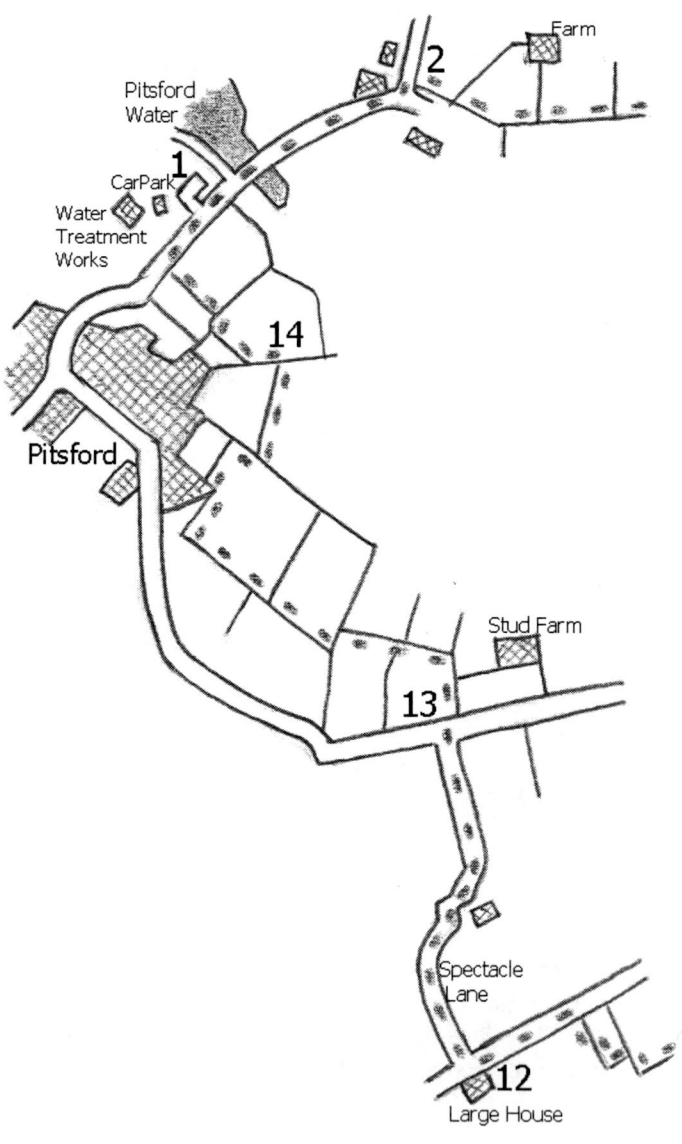

1 Leave by the path through the hedge gap at the lower end of the car park,

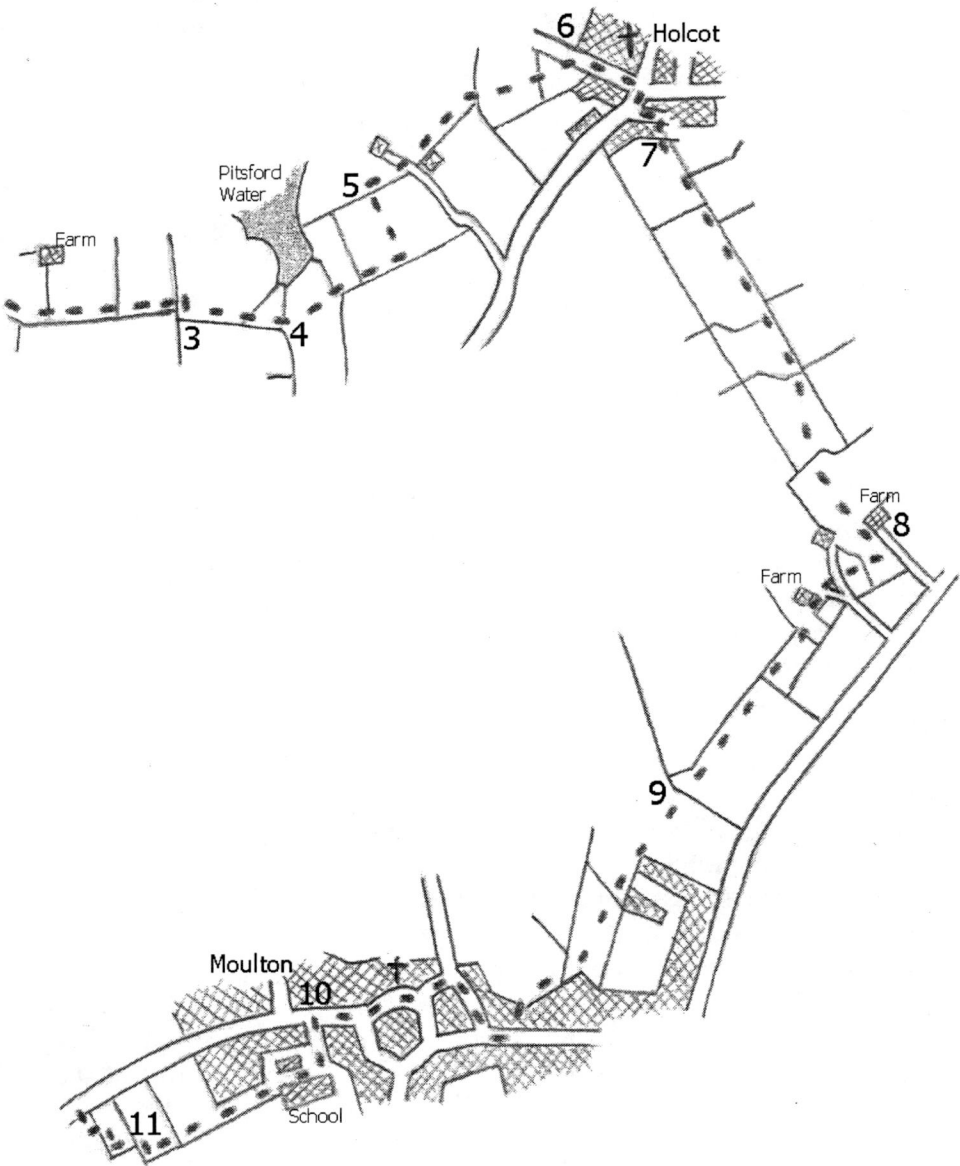

carry on through the angler's car park and turn left out of the gate over the causeway. Continue ahead uphill between fences and fork left at the junction. Go past one gate and bear left through the next, marked by arrow discs.

10 Spectacle Lane completed from the previous Page

2 Turn immediate right and follow this right hand field edge as it veers right then left into the corner. Go through the boundary and keep direction to the next corner go over the footbridge and through the kissing gate. Continue direction through two more kissing gates and turn right for 40yds into the field corner.

3 Turn left back to the original direction along the right hand field edge. At the bottom of the slope cross the footbridge and bear left on a track which should be visible within any crop, to a less substantial two sleeper footbridge in the trees.

4 Bear left over the field ahead parallel with the telegraph poles, the field may be under cultivation but a track should be well marked. Pass through the gates and over the footbridge in the dip, continue on the right hand field edge and turn left over the field at the marker post (a track should be visible).

5 Cross the stile at the signpost and turn right. Bear slight left in the corner on the broad grassy track between the hedge and the fence, bear right at the signpost in the dip, turn left over the bridge and follow the right hand field edge over a stile and keep direction to the road.

6 Turn right into Holcot. At the crossroads turn right along Moulton Road, left into Back Lane and immediate right across the stile at the footpath sign.

7 Bear left between the barn and the hedge; follow the left hand field edge over the stile in the corner. Continue ahead between hedge and fence and carry on through the undergrowth past the pond in this corner. From the next boundary follow the farm track on a right hand diagonal over the field around the pond to a stile 100yds left of the opposite corner. Go straight on over the field and keep direction over a double stile/footbridge along the left hand field edge.

8 At the far end of the farm turn right in front of a metal gate; follow the fence and cross a stile. Carry on across the field and bridge, from the road bear left over the grass. Go through a narrow then a wide gate and cross the farmyard; bear left in front of the final barn, turn right over the stile and walk down the right hand field edge. Keep direction across a stile and a brick bridge near the next corner; go through a gate, over a narrow field corner and step over the stile.

9 Keep direction ahead over the open field, from the corner just before the telegraph poles take a right hand diagonal to the jutting out corner and bear left on the left hand field edge. In the corner follow the enclosed path and bear left into Moulton. Turn right along Overstone Road, at the 'Give Way' sign turn right into Chater Street, bear left into Church Street. Walk past the 'Artichoke' and go straight on along Church Hill past the church; continue right/straight on at the junction.

10 Turn left opposite the 'Telegraph' into Pound Lane and go into Moulton School gates; turn right and follow the marker discs through the school grounds, turn right at mathematics then left through the sunken path. Keep direction along the hedge lined track at the rear of the houses, over a stile and down the left hand edge of the next three fields.

11 Turn right in the corner for 60yds, turn left over the double stile and continue on the field edge to the corner. Turn right and walk up to the stile on the left, step over and carry on with the hedge now on the right; join the road and turn left.

12 At the top of the rise turn right into Spectacle Lane, follow this road/byway over the footbridge by the ford and keep going as it goes right then left uphill past a farm, all the way to the road.

13 Cross the stile ahead, go along the fenced path and follow it left in the corner. Turn left at the top then immediate right on the field edge. Keep on the left hand edge of this vast field around several corners; the track eventually goes through a narrow hedge gap in the top corner.

14 Turn left at the marker post and follow the field edge to the kissing gate. Turn right along the path back to the car park and your vehicle.

Notes

The 'Walking Close to' Series

Peterborough
The Nene near Peterborough
The Nene Valley Railway near Wansford
The Nene near Oundle
The Torpel Way (Peterborough to Stamford)
The Great North Road near Stilton

Cambridge
Grafham Water (Huntingdonshire)
The Great Ouse in Huntingdonshire
The Cam and the Granta near Cambridge
Newmarket
The Isle of Ely

Northamptonshire/Warwickshire
The Nene near Thrapston
The Nene near Wellingborough
The River Ise near Kettering
The Nene near Northampton
Pitsford Water
Rockingham Forest
Daventry and North West Northamptonshire
Rugby

Leicestershire
Rutland Water
Eye Brook near Uppingham
The Soar near Leicester
Lutterworth
The Vale of Belvoir (North Leicestershire)
Melton Mowbray
The Welland near Market Harborough

Lincolnshire
The Welland near Stamford
Bourne and the Deepings
South Lincolnshire

Suffolk
Lavenham in Suffolk
Bury St Edmunds
The Stour near Sudbury
The Orwell near Ipswich
Dedham Vale
Stowmarket
Clare, Cavendish and Haverhill
Southwold and the Suffolk Coast

Hampshire
Romsey and the Test Valley

Essex/Hertfordshire
Hertford and the Lee Valley
The Colne near Colchester
Epping Forest (North London)
Chelmsford

Wiltshire/Bath
The Avon near Bath
Bradford-on-Avon
Corsham and Box
The Avon near Chippenham

Bedfordshire/Milton Keynes
The Great Ouse near Bedford
The Great Ouse North of Milton Keynes
Woburn Abbey

Somerset & Devon
Cheddar Gorge
Glastonbury and the City of Wells
The Quantock Hills
The East Devon Coast (Sidmouth, Branscombe and Beer)
Exmouth and East Devon

Norfolk
The Norfolk Broads (Northern Area)
The Norfolk Broads (Southern Area)
The Great Ouse near King's Lynn
North West Norfolk (Hunstanton and Wells)
Thetford Forest
North Norfolk (Cromer and Sheringham)

Nottinghamshire
Sherwood Forest
The Dukeries (Sherwood Forest)
The Trent near Nottingham

Oxfordshire/Berkshire
The Thames near Oxford
The Cotswolds near Witney
The Vale of White Horse
Woodstock and Blenheim Palace
Henley-on-Thames
Banbury
The River Pang (Reading/Newbury)
The Kennet near Newbury

Cumbria
Cartmel and Southern Lakeland

Hereford and Worcester
The Severn near Worcester
South West Herefordshire (Hay-on-Wye and Kington)
The Malvern Hills